Sharing Time With Nana

How to write a book with your grandchild

Have fun!   Create a legacy!

Suggested age range-- 5 years to 12 years

Margaret O'Connell

Acknowledgements

Thanks to Mary and Rahm, Katie, Mary Elizabeth and my Red Hat friends

copyright© 2013 2nd edition

copyright© 2012

All rights reserved. Clipart from Dreamstime.com and CanStockPhoto.com. No part of this book may be reproduced or utilized in any form or by any means, electronic or mechanical, including photocopying, recording, or by any information storage or retrieval system, without permission in writing from the author or publisher.

TABLE OF CONTENTS

Materials & General Directions   Page   4

PREWRITING SECTION

Storytelling	Page 9
Brainstorming	Page 17
Graphic Organizers	Page 23

WRITING SECTION

Drafting	Page 51
Expanding/Revising	Page 57
Proofreading	Page 63
Publishing	Page 67
Illustrating	Page 71
Binding	Page 75
Sharing	Page 79

Flip Book storyteller practice	Page 81
Directions for Grab Bag Stories	Page 103

Appendix

Grab Bag cards
About the Authors page
Comments and Compliments page

Materials and General directions to Nana

1. Gather materials:
    a. Pencils
    b. Scissors
    c. Glue or tape
    d. Markers or crayons
    e. 5 lunch-size bags
    f. Paper for your final product
    g. Card stock or a file folder to cut to make the cover----you could keep your work in the file folder until you're ready for your cover. You will want two—one for each of you.

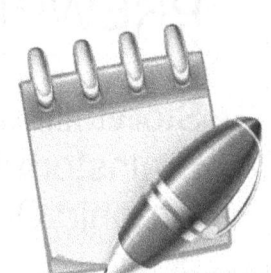

2. Nana may want to read through this book before the bookmaking meeting with your grandchild.
3. Follow the first direction of the Flip Book section. (in case you want to do the cutting and **put the scissors away.**) You will make sure these pages **ARE NOT** cut out of the book like the Grab Bag section.)
4. Follow the first three directions of the Grab Bag section (same **caution with the scissors.**) These cards **ARE** to be cut out of the book.

INTRODUCTION

Congratulations on wanting to enjoy a special experience with your grandchild!

This is a process that you will be able to follow and have a few good laughs with your grandchild. Once you finish one book, you'll want to do another.

The book is broken down into easy-to-follow steps. **At the beginning of each chapter is a coloring page for the grandchild to color.** It has the title of the chapter on the coloring page. This is also a good opportunity for some vocabulary building.

There are lines on the back of most pages in this handbook for you to take notes on your ideas and stories.

I know you will have a great experience with your grandchild.

Enjoy the legacy item you've created for many years to come!

Storytelling

PREWRITING

STORYTELLING

The first part of writing is called prewriting. This is a fun time for both grandparent and grandchild. You can talk about any special interests. Try some "what if" or "imagine if" ideas. (Remember---you are just talking---not writing yet!)

This is another way of saying,

"Let's talk about………
    let's talk about your pet….
    let's talk about your favorite part of the school day…
    let's talk about your best friend…
    let's talk about your hobby…

    OR
    what would you do if…
    you found a magic coin?
    met a giant?
    found a fairy in your garden?
    you were president?
    you changed places with mom or dad?
    you could be really, really tall or really, really small?

At this point, Nana could model some descriptive words----not to correct the child, but just to model some great vocabulary. Have fun with this!

Tell several stories to each other with these story starters or any other ones you may like better.

STORYTELLING ACTIVITIES

A couple of activities that kids enjoy doing to make up their stories are Grab Bag Stories and Flip Book Stories. See directions at the back of the book on how to set up Grab Bag Stories and how to use the Flip Book pages at the back of the book.

The Grab Bag stories are generated by drawing a card out of each bag with either a picture or words written on them. There's a bag for each component of the story: who, where, when, what happened.

Once you draw a card from each bag, you have the basics for your story. It can be silly, funny or very imaginative. Together make up your story. Take turns starting the story. Add to each other's suggestion for the story. Have fun! Have some laughs. Be creative!

Throw the cards back in the appropriate bags. Draw out some new cards and make up a new story. Try it a few times to get in the mode of creating a new story.

You can do it in many combinations:

    take turns drawing a card and adding your part;

    take cards and just swap one component of the story;

    after you try it enough times, each person takes one from each bag and you make your own story.

In a similar manner, use the Flip Book at the back of the book to create stories. Flip each part of the page up to the fold line you created to make a short story. One portion can stay constant and move the other two. Any and all combinations are fun! Nana may have to read these parts to the grandchild depending on the age and or skill level of the grandchild.

The first one might say: The elephant took a walk at the mall.

OR The elephant played the guitar at city hall.

OR A witch landed a spaceship in the park...etc...

Then create your story from the pages you flipped over. Have some fun!! Have some giggles!!

BRAINSTORMING

The next part is what I would call brainstorming. For this part you would list all the topics about which you could tell the story. This is the time to generate possibilities.

You might go back to some of the ideas you had when you pulled characters and story elements out of the bags while making up the Grab Bag stories. You might prefer the ideas you generated when you were making up stories with the Flip Book pages. You may have favorite animals, hobbies, superheroes or special talents.

Start listing the topics that pop into your heads. You may get 10 things down. Just jot the ideas down on paper that might generate story possibilities. Don't start finding fault with an idea or even expanding on it yet---just start listing them. Review your list and decide which ones are the most appealing.

Go over each one and see which ones you select as the top three. When the both of you agree, pick the top one. The other two may be your next books!

Okay, let's write a story about your topic that would be fun.

Then, brainstorm:

1. the characters that might be in it,
2. where it's going to take place,
3. when the story would take place,
4. what's going to happen

Include all of these categories as starting possibilities when you're creating your story together.

Now that you have some ideas and you've done some practice stories together, it's time to craft your book. Cherish this creative time that you've spent together.

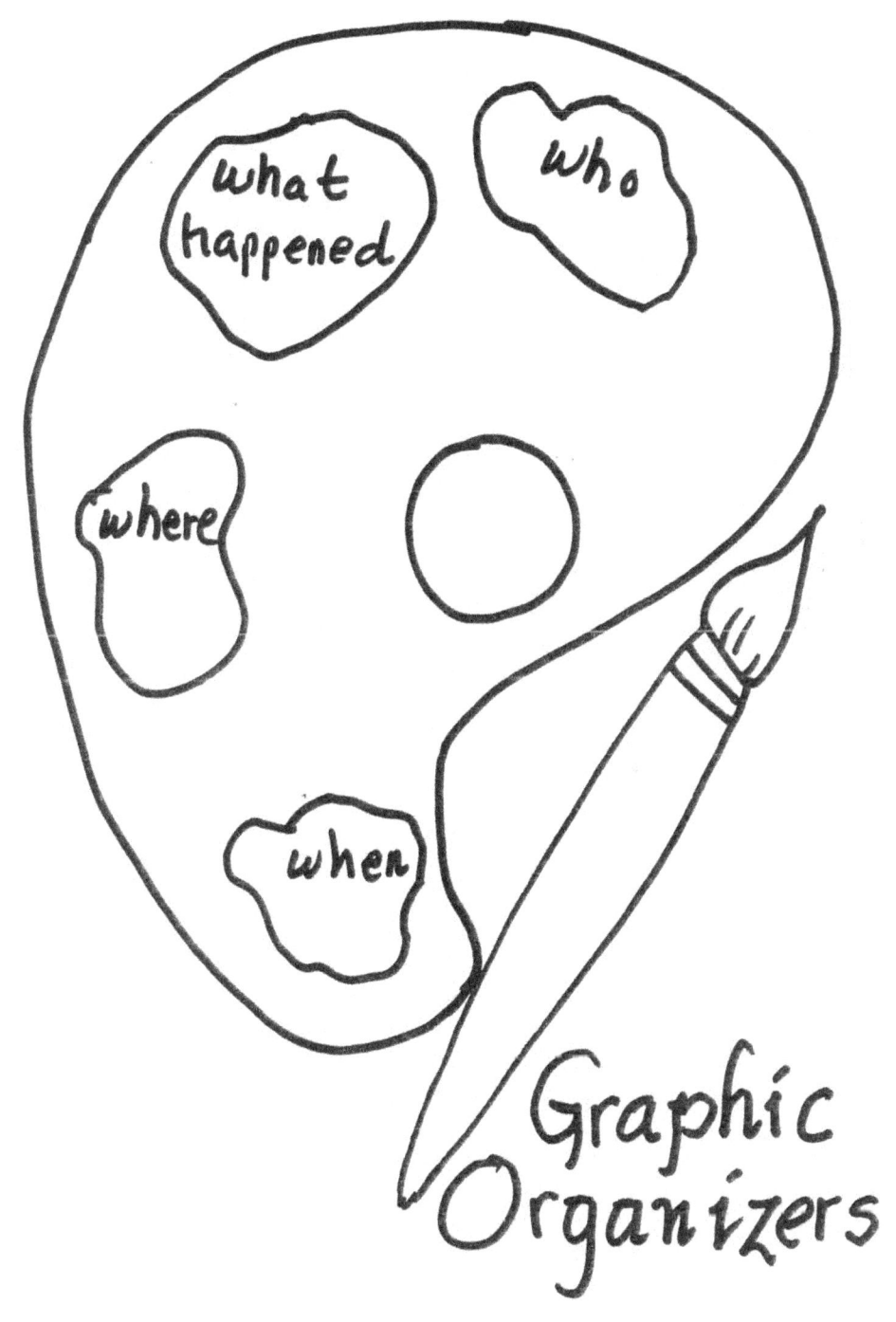

GRAPHIC ORGANIZERS

You've had some good laughs by now. So let's start putting the story together. This is where you start doing some writing. This next section is called "Using Graphic Organizers."

These are simple diagrams to get your ideas down on paper in a way to help you organize your thoughts. By using one of these formats, you can add to any section any time before you start actually writing your story.

Graphic Organizers may be a new term for Nana. It's easier than the outline format you learned in school. Your grandchild is probably familiar with this term. Sometimes teachers call it a story web or a story map.

A simple way to start is with three boxes in a row labeled beginning, middle, end, especially with younger children.

Sometimes we use a picture of a hamburger with the bun on the bottom, the burger in the middle, and the bun on the top as the beginning, middle and end of your story.

Or you could use a train with three cars—as another way to organize your beginning, middle and end.

Use a sample organizer at the end of this chapter or draw your own.

I've drawn several different organizers. I didn't use an artist or my computer. **I wanted to show you that you or your grandchild can draw an organizer**. It doesn't have to be perfect.

My favorite way is to draw circles or ovals because it's the simplest. Draw circles or ovals in random order. Draw lines off each circle to add ideas.

Label each of the circles with the traditional who, what happened, when, and where. I'm not listing "why" as a separate part because it falls into the "what happened" at this age. The nice thing about this graphic organizer is that you can add little lines to each circle as thoughts pop up! They don't need to be sentences yet.

For example, as your grandchild tells about where the story takes place, you can add his or her details. You may add some of your own at the same time as well. The time might be mentioned in the telling --- so you can add that detail to the "when" circle and not disrupt the train of thought.

Some character details may also emerge, maybe one character is skinny or extra tall, so add those details now! Where does your action take place? On a plane? In a car? In the country? In a haunted house? In a cave? At a ranch?

You can see that if any of these locations came up, it might add details to characters or to the time of day or night? time of year? ---just add to the appropriate circle.

Your story will probably have more than one "who" ---the hero or heroine--- as well as some friendly or problem characters. You can just add another circle to describe them and their connections to the story.

Once you have the basics in each circle with a few added details, go back and look at each circle and see if you have enough information at each element of the organizer. Take some time to see if you want to add some more details to any part of it. Or you might want to eliminate or change some ideas. Just do it here and now.

It's a very flexible format. It's not like you have to worry about changing anything in your description or that it's written in stone.

I would start with the "what happens" part. It is what's generally going to generate the story and that could take a little more activity. So you start drawing lines off this circle and add appropriate ideas.

Now go back and review what you have at "the who". Does it fit with the action? Should we add or delete anything? Check out the rest of the major elements.
You can add all the details you like.

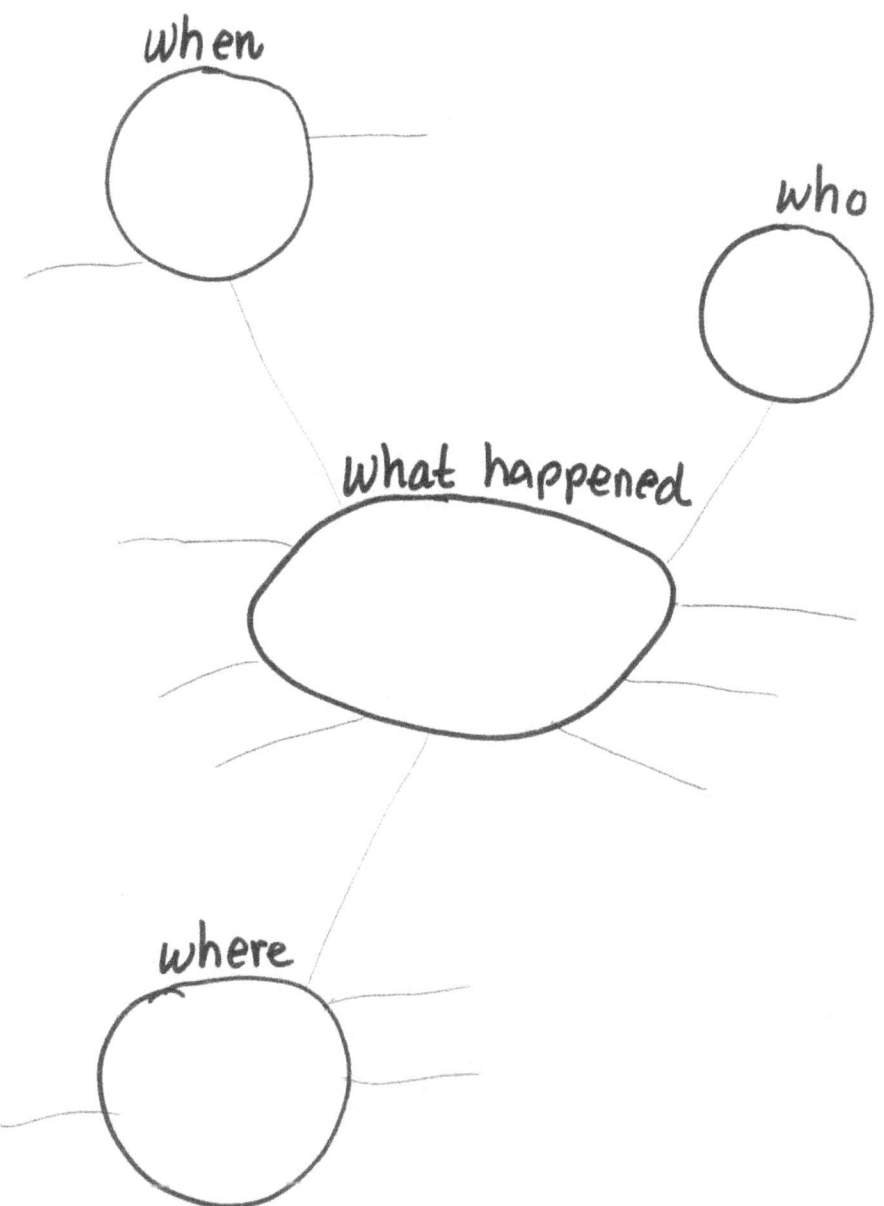

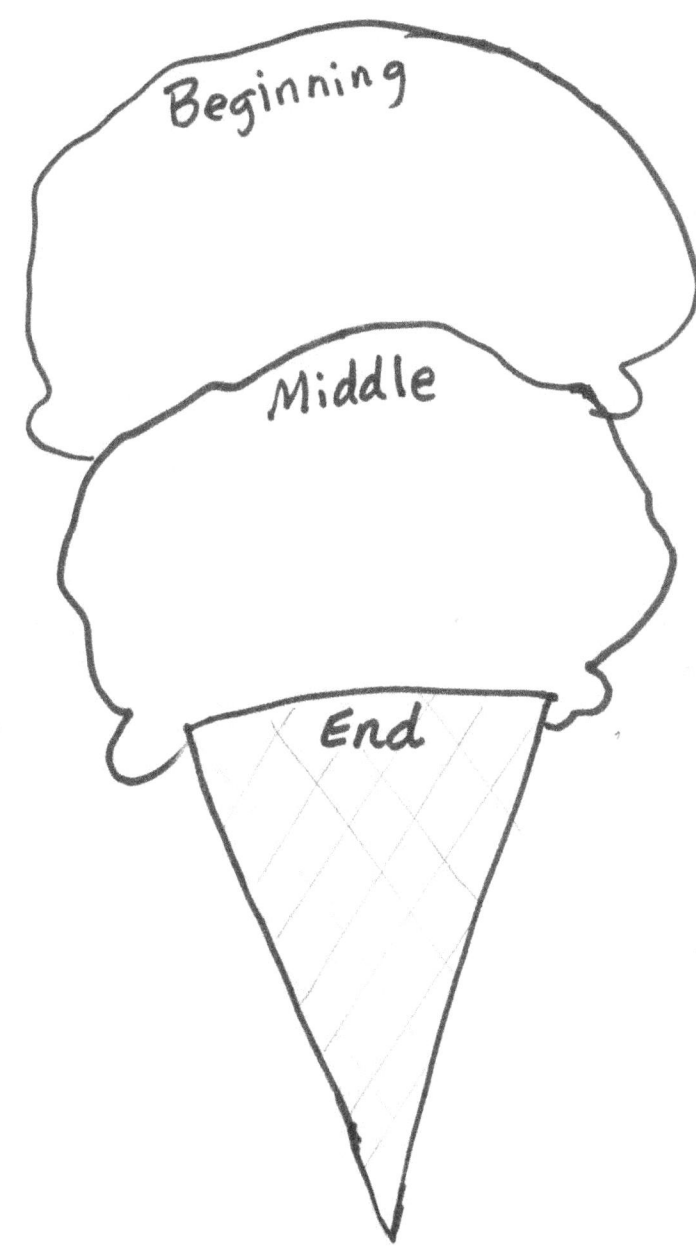

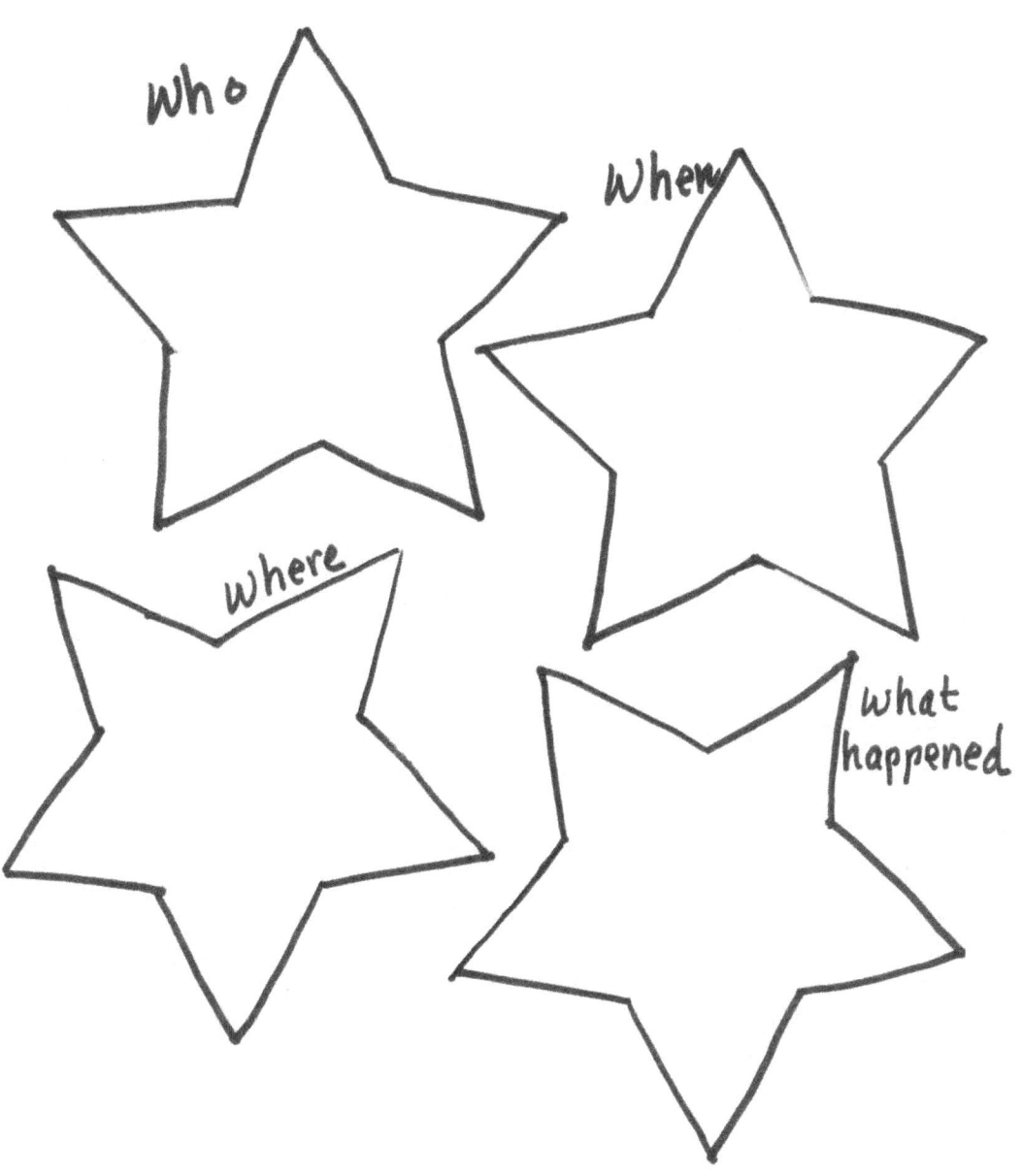

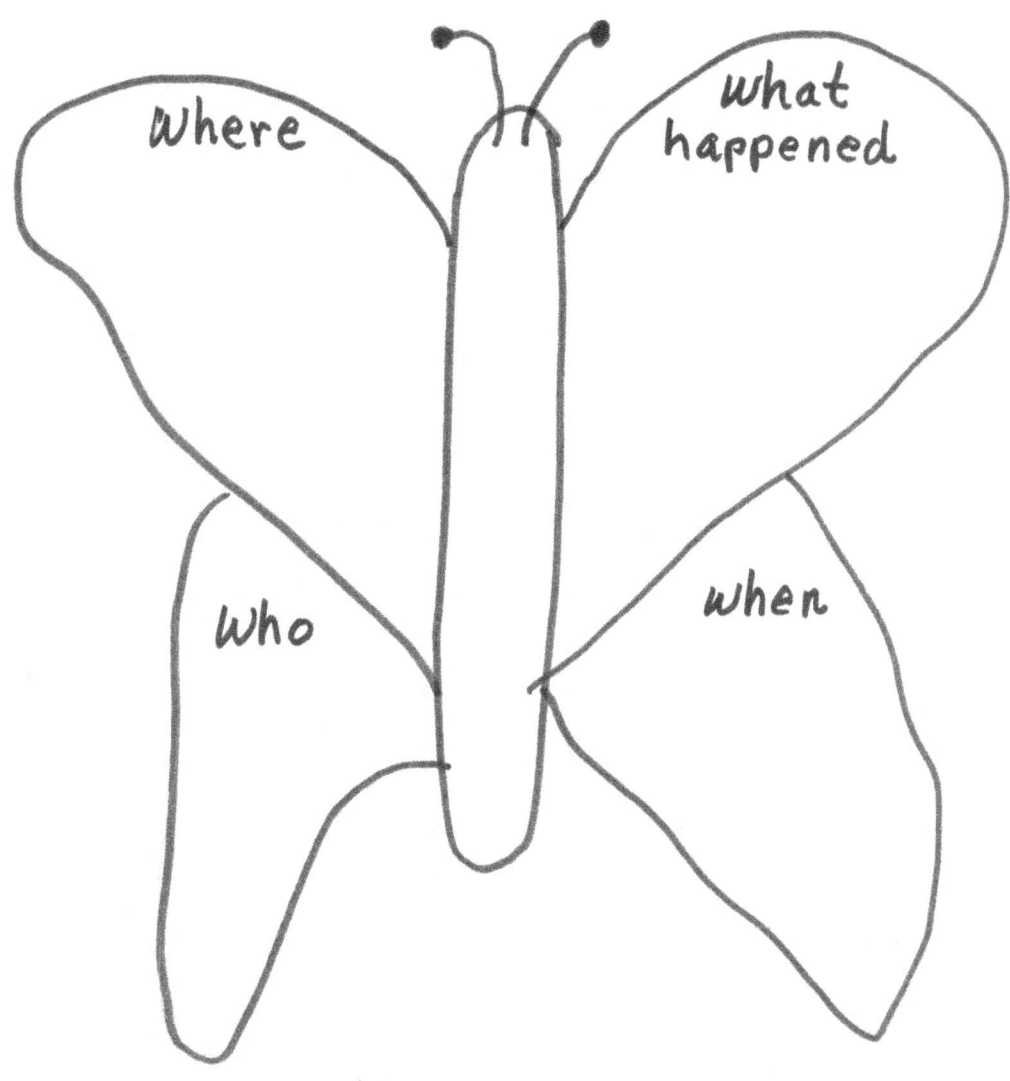

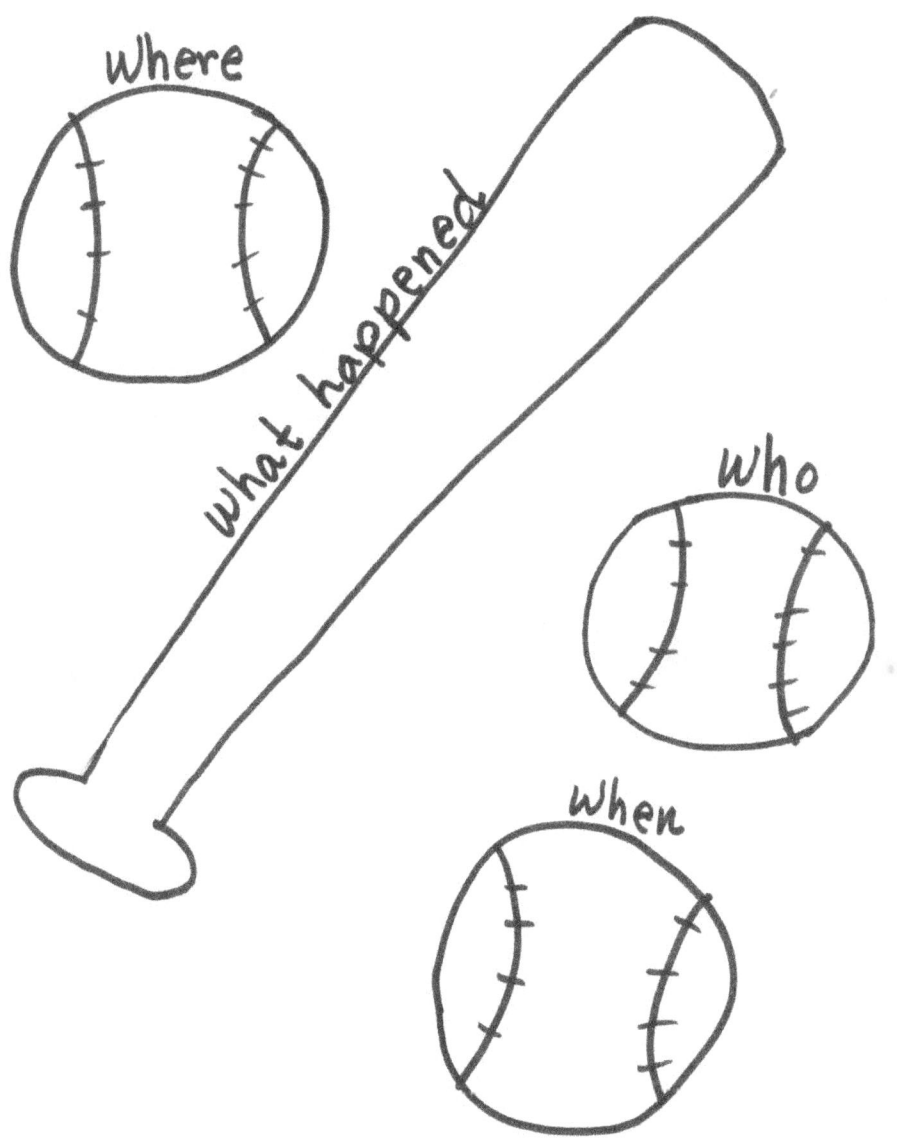

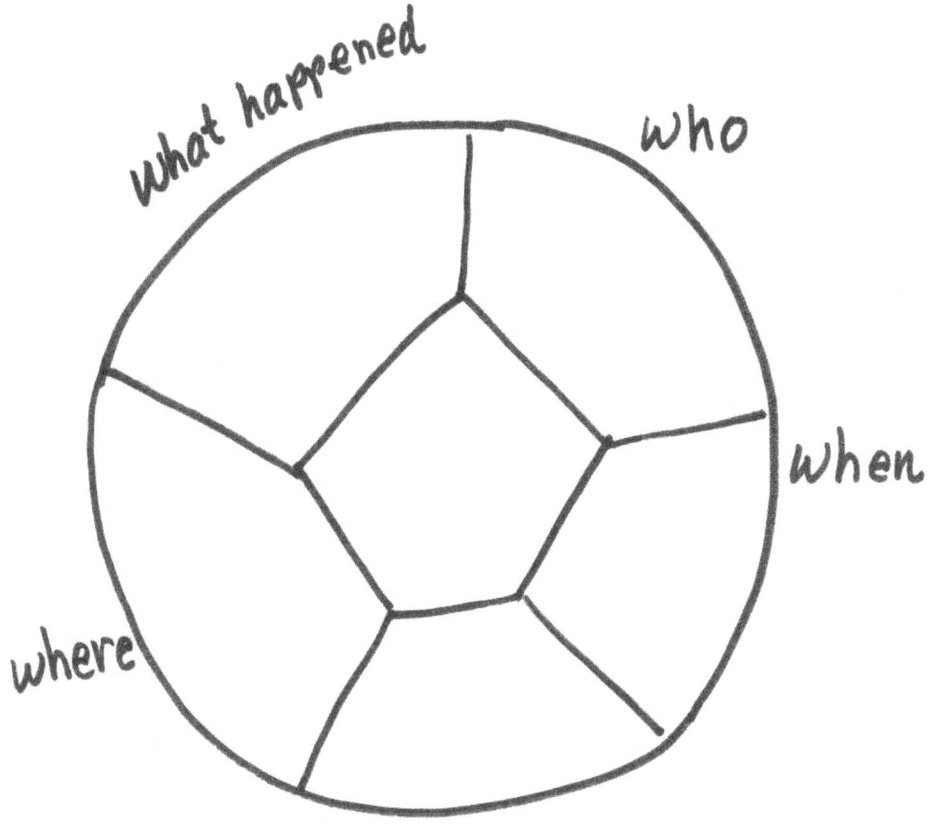

Drafting

WRITING

DRAFTING

The next section is drafting your story. Now we're finally starting the writing. Using your skeleton story or framework from the graphic organizer, the story will flow together.

You've done most of the creative part of writing your book. You have done a lot of "fun stuff" to get to this point.

The pre-writing steps of brainstorming and storytelling led you to the graphic organizer.

The drafting is really going to be much simpler to do when you start writing because the framework of the story is on your graphic organizer.

Depending on the age of the child, the grandchild could start the actual writing on paper. Nana, don't make this a chore for the child. It might be easier and go smoother if you do the writing at this point.

I always use what I call the "sloppy copy" when starting the writing. This simply means using lined paper and skipping every other line. This format makes it easier to make additions and deletions to your story. Cross-outs and erasures are no problem!!

This format saves time and promotes success.

Some kids resist this format at first because they think it should look perfect. It doesn't have to look perfect from the beginning. The **sloppy copy** provides the perfect place to do your revising, which is the next step.

Think about a title for your book. At this point it may just be a working title. You can always change it when you're ready to publish.

Revising & Expanding

REVISING AND EXPANDING

When you've finished writing your sloppy copy, it's time to do some revising and expanding. You probably don't need much work on the story line because you've done all the preliminary steps...maybe a few interesting details.

It's a good idea for both of you to agree to changes. This is the time to do any expanding on any ideas that seem appropriate.

Nana, you might want to know the state standards criteria for assessing writing in school. They are similar in every state. All these should be age appropriate.

In revising, (using State Standards) ask yourself and grandchild, "Did we include…?
an easy-to-follow sequence/ or fluency
descriptive words
good grammar
not too much dialogue
organization
conventions such as spelling and punctuation

You still want this to be a creative collaboration of both Nana and grandchild---not all in Nana's perfect style and language.

You're almost done…….the fun's not over….

Have your grandchild perform the **honor** of writing the words "**THE END**" on the last page of your book. They love to do that!

Add an Authors' Page. I've provided a sample for you in the appendix.

Write a short passage about each of you. You may want to include: some facts about your family, your hobbies, where you live (not your address), what you like to do with your friends.

The grandchild may want to include age, school name, grade and the names of two or three friends. These are fun facts that the grandchild will appreciate in a few years, when he looks at the book again. (See sample Author's Page at the back of this book. Make a photocopy or create your own.)

Add a photo of both of you together.

Add a page at the end called "Comments and Compliments". When anyone reads your book, invite them to write something positive, especially to the grandchild. (See sample at the back of the book.) Don't forget to write your comments in each other's books. You might want more than one of these pages---maybe three to five more. **Expect lots of kudos!!!**

Proofreading

PROOFREADING

Still using your sloppy copy, check your writing for grammar, punctuation and spelling.

The child can help with some of the corrections. You may **not** want to take out some of the cute phrasing that the child may use, even if it's not totally grammatically correct for this purpose. This is **not** an assignment for a grade.

Depending on the age and skill level of the child, he or she can help with the proofreading. The grandchild can help with simple things like beginning a sentence with a capital letter and ending with the period or question mark. Child may also help check for commas and check spelling as appropriate.

Nana might make those changes so the child shouldn't feel like Nana is correcting every little thing they're saying.

As you're proofreading, determine where you're going to end each page. Using a red marker, put a dot (a "**stop dot**") at the end of a sentence to indicate that's all for that page.

An easy idea to keep in mind is "Would this make a good illustration?" If yes, put a red stop dot there. Some pages may have several sentences---some may just have one sentence.

Three or four pages of your writing may yield ten or fifteen pages of a children's book. That just means more fun drawing illustrations.

Publishing

PUBLISHING

Now it's time to copy your story from the sloppy copy to your fresh paper. You could write it on the pages where you plan to do your illustrations or write on plain paper and glue the illustrations to the written page. Remember, copy your text to the red stop dot, then start a new page.

Depending again on the age of the child, the child could write it or you could use a word processing program on your computer.

Create your cover. Title your book. Illustrate the cover. Remember you need two copies—one for each of you.

If you want the illustration and the writing on the same page without gluing the illustration to written page, do the following:
1. Draw the illustration (don't color it…yet) on the page with the writing.
2. Then make two photocopies of each page.
3. Next, color the illustrations on photocopies. (two copies so that you will each have a copy of the finished book.)

Now you have two copies of the collaborated book. **One legacy item for each of you!**

ILLUSTRATING

Illustrating is often the favorite part for the kids!! It's always a fun part.

If you want the illustration and the writing on the same page without gluing the illustration to a written page, do the following:

1. Draw the illustration (don't color it ...yet) on the page with the writing.
2. Then make two photocopies of each page.
3. Next, color the illustrations on photocopies. (two copies so that you will each have a copy of the finished book.)

Use your favorite medium to add drawings to a story -- markers, colored pencils, crayons, photos and computer-generated artwork. (Some artwork is free and some online sites charge a fee.) Clipart is very helpful, it makes things go a little faster but the child's drawings are always cute. That's fine. You can do the illustrations together. The grandchild could start. You could add something or you could start one to which they could add some things. However you feel comfortable. However it seems to flow will work for you both.

You could take turns doing one page and the child doing another page. Nana might do the first and last page and grandchild does the others--- whatever combination feels right or makes sense at the time. Of course, it is always changeable. If you're doing your illustrating on the computer, you can just print two copies.

Binding

BINDING

Assemble all of the pages. Don't forget your Authors Page and your Comments and Compliments Pages!

Lots of options here:
1. Make a cover for each book and staple it together.
2. Copy stores do comb binding for about two dollars.
3. Copy stores do plastic spiral binding or coil binding for about three dollars.
4. Some office supply stores do a hardcover binding for about ten dollars. They send it out and you have to wait a few days.

Sharing

Would you like to share your book with anyone?
Draw them here.

SHARING

Now your wonderful books are complete!!! They look great, don't they?

Now show them off to family and friends!!

You shared a great experience with your grandchild and you both have great memories of your time together. The bonus is that you each have a great item that created bonding memories every time you look at it.

Your grandchild will have the same response for many years to come. This is a treasure for the grandchild to pass on to **their children.**

You might plan your next book together.

Congratulate yourselves for spending this time together and creating this book!

Directions for Flip Book

Do you remember those fun books as kids that had all different animals? You might have a lion's head, a hippo's body and a monkey's tail. You could flip any part and create a new animal. Well, that's what you're going to do with these story starters.

1. Cut each page on the dotted line from the outside edge of the page to the beginning of the first word so you **create three flaps.** (The printing margins won't allow the dotted line to go to the edge of the page.) You should start at the edge of the page cutting toward the binding.

2. Then flip the flaps in random order to create lots of new sentences as story starters. Sometimes the combinations are just silly. For example, an elephant flew on a broom in the park.

3. Let your imaginations go wild!! This activity gets the child telling all kinds of stories.

4. You can make up your own parts on the back of the pages, if you're having fun and want to expand the activity.

They can be funny and you will have lots of laughs making up stories.

An elephant

------------------✂------------------✂---------

took a walk

------------------✂------------------✂--------

at the mall

A puppy

------------------------✂------------------------✂--------

ran under a bush

------------------------✂------------------------✂--------

in the park.

An alien

landed a spaceship

in a corn field.

A witch

flew on a broom

over the house.

A boy

played the guitar

at city hall.

A girl

played soccer

at the field.

A clown

---- ✂ ---- ✂ ----

made balloon animals

at the party.

A cat

chased a rabbit

into a hole.

A pilot

landed the plane

at the airport.

A superhero

got a new power

online.

Directions for Grab Bag stories

You need to have five bags. Lunch bags are the easiest size to use. It's fun to use decorated ones, like holiday bags or gift bags.

1. Label each bag. One for each category: who, when, where, what happened, extra fun
2. Before you cut the cards, you might want to draw a line with a crayon or marker down the page. Use a different color for each category. This way when you cut them, you can easily sort. For example, all the "who cards" have a red stripe, all the "when cards" have a green stripe, etc. It will make it easy to put them in the labeled bags.

3. Cut the cards out of the book on the dotted lines.

4. Place the cards in the appropriate bag.
5. Draw one card from each bag.
6. Make up a story using the cards that you drew out the bags
7. It's fun to change just one card and change your story OR Nana and grandchild trade one card with each other and make a new story.

8. HAVE FUN!!!!!

List of Grab Bag Cards

Who cards   Pig, cow, turtle, walrus, koala, zebra, penguin, queen, alligator, octopus

When cards   At noon, at midnight, at Halloween, in the spring, in the winter, in the morning, on January 1, on the 4th of July, at recess, after school

Where cards   At the skateboard park, in the smelly swamp, in the dusty attic, on the slippery roof, under the shade ramada, under the beach umbrella, in the round horse corral, in the giant aquarium, on a bright green fire truck, in a tiny wooden birdhouse

What happened cards   went into a dark cave, went into the haunted house, had a family picnic, climbed a steep mountain, went to school on Saturday, built a fat snowman, built a large sandcastle, mowed the tall grass in the yard, planted a vegetable garden, got in an old rowboat, lifted up by a large bird

Extra fun cards   igloo, watch, rose, cake, x-ray, tent, lemon, jet, baseball, snowman

Appendix

Grab Bag word cards

About the Authors page

Comments and Compliments page

Pig

Cow

Turtle

Walrus

Koala

Zebra

Penguin

Queen

Alligator

Octopus

Igloo

Watch

Rose

Cake

X-ray

Tent

Lemon

Jet

Baseball

Snowman

At noon

At midnight

At Halloween

In the spring

In the winter

In the morning

On January 1

On the 4th of July

At recess

After school

At the skateboard park

----

in the smelly swamp

In the dusty attic

On the slippery roof

Under the shade ramada

Under the beach umbrella

In the round horse corral

In the giant aquarium

By the corner Stop sign

On a bright green
fire truck

In a tiny wooden
birdhouse

Went into a dark cave

Went into the haunted house

Had a family picnic

Climbed a steep mountain

Went to school on Saturday

Built a fat snowman

Built a large sandcastle

Mowed the tall grass in the yard

Planted a vegetable garden

Got in an old row boat

Lifted up by a large bird

About the Authors

Comments and Compliments

www.ingramcontent.com/pod-product-compliance
Lightning Source LLC
Chambersburg PA
CBHW080344170426
43194CB00014B/2681